A Basket of Apples

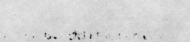

A Basket of Apples

Recollections
—— of ——
Historic Nova Scotia

Text by Harry Bruce

Photography by Chic Harris

Toronto
OXFORD UNIVERSITY PRESS
1982

ACKNOWLEDGEMENTS

I wish to thank the Hon. Victor deB. Oland for granting permission to reproduce the brewery calendar (page 79); Don Oland, marine artist L.B. Jenson, and Bluenose Designs, Halifax, for permission to reproduce Mr Jenson's sketch of *Bluenose II* (page 52); and Eric Ruff, curator, Yarmouth County Museum, for permission to print the photograph of the pioneer communion service (page 25). I am grateful, too, as I have been countless times before, for the help of Shirley Elliott, chief of the legislative library in Halifax. Finally, my wife Penny. If she had not compiled the research, typed it, checked it, and periodically dumped piles of it in my lap, I'd never have met my editorial deadlines, and this basket of apples would remain untasted.

Title page: Herring gull

Perfect take-off: Ornithologists know the herring gull as Larus argentatus. *Others call it a mackerel gull, big white gull, gray gull, blue gull, bluey gull, bluey, lookabout, or just a sea-gull. The bird's the same all over Nova Scotia but its ancient nicknames change from cove to cove.*

Canadian Cataloguing in Publication Data

Main entry under title:
  A Basket of apples

ISBN 0-19-540393-2

1. Nova Scotia – Social life and customs. 2. Nova Scotia – History.   I. Bruce, Harry, 1934-
II. Harris, Chic.

FC2318.B37	971.6	C82-094581-1
F1037.B37		

Designed by FORTUNATO AGLIALORO (*STUDIO 2 GRAPHICS*)

© Oxford University Press (Canadian Branch) 1982
ISBN 0-19-540393-2

1 2 3 4-5 4 3 2

Printed in Hong Kong by
EVERBEST PRINTING COMPANY LIMITED

INTRODUCTION

Not long ago, a little girl in Halifax, Nova Scotia, found a yellow balloon bearing a message on a pink tag. The message was that another little girl had released the balloon in Gardner, Massachusetts. Ocean winds had whipped it 450 miles to a tree in the Halifax kid's backyard. After she wrote to the Gardner girl, a Massachusetts newspaper announced, 'Gardner Balloon Settles in Nova Scotia'. The paper also explained that Halifax was 'the capital of the island of Nova Scotia,' and 'the island is due east of New Brunswick.'

If the balloon had not been such a breezy, pleasing example of the handy communications with New England that Nova Scotia has enjoyed for more than two centuries, the newspaper's boner might have inspired familiar Canadian bleating about Yankee ignorance of Canadian fact. That would have been a shame. For if Nova Scotia is not an island, it is *almost* an island. On a map, the land that connects it to New Brunswick looks like a mooring line that might snap in a storm, allowing the weather to sweep the whole province out to sea. The line is actually seventeen miles thick, but that's not so much when you consider that the massively intricate Nova

Scotia coast winds for 4,625 miles. That's longer than the breadth of the whole continent.

Nova Scotia, in short, is so close to being an island that her people are like island people, and islanders have certain things in common. For one thing, the sea dominates their history. The story of any inhabited island is one of voyages and vessels, of comings and goings by water, of pursuing fish in the sea and trade goods over the sea, of fighting, dying, and thriving on the dark ocean. Even the folklore of islands looks seaward, towards eerie lights and apparitions, the wails of the long-drowned, wandering ghost ships, and blazing phantom ships. Islands tend to be a shade more spooky than the mainland.

With the sea surrounding islanders, and the sky above them, with sea and sky meaning the difference between profit and loss, or sometimes between life and death, island people are weather-watchers. Weather is like an initiation into a secret society. Together, the members face both the pleasures and terrors of weather in a clearly outlined and plainly vulnerable spot. One could make too much of the comparison, but islanders during

storms are like Londoners during the blitz of the Second World War. They share a sense of community, pride of place, and something that wavers between fatalism and self-sufficiency. *We're all in this together. We'll get by. We always did before, didn't we?* Finally, islanders have long memories. No one is so homesick as an islander who's moved for good to a mainland city.

Nova Scotians, in all these respects, are islanders; and they're deeply conscious of their 'island's' history. A Toronto journalist has suggested that one reason why French-English relations are rotten is that, in all Canada, only the people of Quebec have an abiding sense of their own history. He is off the mark. Nova Scotians know in their bellies that they've inherited an epic past; and indeed, so far as European settlement goes, that their past predates even Quebec's. They know that they are *who* they are because, for centuries, they and their forebears have been stuck out there beside the great shipping lanes of the North Atlantic, and caught in the bloody clash of nations.

They know why the French founded Louisbourg, why the English founded Halifax, why the Scots settled eastern Nova Scotia, why the New Englanders came, and why the Acadians left. What other province, incidentally, can boast a story so heart-breaking as the expulsion of the Acadians? Not every Nova Scotian can be precise about names and dates, but words with historical reverberations echo in their heads: privateer, pirate, schooner, corvette, convoy, *Titanic*, West Indies trade, salt fish, rum-running, explosion, responsible government, Joseph Howe...

If you wander into the small, elegant library at Province House, Halifax, you'll find yourself in the room in which young Joe Howe, in 1835, beat a libel charge by making a six-hour speech that became a landmark in forensic eloquence. It not only got him off, it also established the right of the press to attack corruption in colonial administrations. More than that, it launched Howe on a political career that culminated thirteen years later in Nova Scotia's achieving responsible government. His biographer, J.W. Longley, wrote, 'Never, after 1848, was the idea entertained in any province of British America, having a constitution, that an administration could hold office an hour longer than it had the confidence of the people represented in the popular branch.' The fight had been fierce but never lethal. Hangings, riots, and the burning of public buildings accompanied the same fight in central Canada; and when the movement to form the Canadian confederation began, many Nova Scotians opposed union with such uncivilized, western barbarians.

In 1867, however, Nova Scotia did become one of the four founding provinces of Canada; or, as most Nova Scotians felt, it was railroaded into a new nation. Sometimes, even now, attacks on 'Upper Canada' in the Nova Scotia press make you think a time-machine has plunged you back into the 1860s. Sometimes, even now, the words of Joe Howe are invoked in the Legislature. In the taverns of Nova Scotia, men still talk of his oratory, his popularity, his drinking habits, his 'womanizing'. It is as though he died last week rather than 109 years ago. No, Quebec is not the only province in which history still counts.

Nova Scotians share a dream of the past: the province was once rich; the towns were self-sufficient; great industries hummed in the coal and steel districts; great wooden vessels scudded off to sea and returned with treasure from exotic ports; and great families built graceful mansions that defied the ocean weather. Ah yes, the Age of Sail, preserved in an amber haze. But it was stolen away. Technology stole it. Upper Canadian economic clout stole it. It was stolen by politicans who sucked Nova Scotia into the Canadian confederation with promises that later politicians betrayed. There's truth in the dream, but even among Nova Scotians there's rarely been a consensus on exactly how much truth. No less a figure than Robert L. Stanfield, the most respected Nova Scotian politician of our time, once allowed that he couldn't see much evidence, aside from some handsome houses on the South Shore, that Nova Scotians had ever been rolling in wealth. ('I accept the wooden ships and iron men,' he also said, 'but those who complain about the decline in the work ethic should recall that even in those great days it was frequently necessary to ply men with rum before they would work.')

The point, however, is not how much accuracy lies in the dream of the lost golden age. It is simply that, way back in the northeast-

ern corner of a Nova Scotian's mind, he derives pride from it. It's alive.

Nova Scotians are history-conscious in a more personal way as well. Family history counts down here, and speaking of family, my father, Charles Bruce, a Nova Scotian who spent most of his life in Toronto, once wrote about 'Companionship in Time'. Many Nova Scotians still have that. 'More and more,' he wrote, 'I am becoming convinced that the only real history of any country is cross-roads history. The fact that old Sandy Cummings helped to put out a fire in a Micmac encampment, while the braves were away, and so was safe, in person and possessions, for life. That, seventy-five years later, Reuben McIntosh used to wade out to his whaleboat in water up to his shoulders, instead of taking his rowboat to it. And that when rheumatism got him it really got him. So bad that he couldn't turn over in bed, and the young people of the place would take turns coming in to help Aunt Panthy.

'This kind of history is important to us. Local history. Hearsay history. This is the stuff in which the heart of humanity beats forever.'

The photography of Chic Harris is the work of a man who knows that in Nova Scotia two kinds of history still matter: the companionship of time, and a royal decree that echoes through generations; cross-roads history, and cannon-and-treaty history. A retired chemist from Montreal, Harris chose to splurge his late-blooming talent as a photographer on Nova Scotia. He's eighty-one. He knows the importance of not wasting the time of his life; and in this basket of his photographic apples from historic Nova Scotia, not one is rotten.

Harry Bruce
Halifax, April 1982

BIBLIOGRAPHY

Books

Bird, Michael J. *The Town That Died*. London, Souvenir Press, 1962.

Bird, Will R. *Off-Trail in Nova Scotia*. Toronto, The Ryerson Press, 1956.
– *This is Nova Scotia*. Toronto, The Ryerson Press, 1950.

Brebner, John Bartlet. *The Neutral Yankees of Nova Scotia*. Toronto, McClelland and Stewart Limited, 1969.

Bruce, Charles. *Mulgrave Road*. Toronto, Macmillan, 1951.

Bruce, Harry. *Lifeline*. Toronto, Macmillan of Canada, 1977.
– *R.A.: The Story of R.A. Jodrey, Entrepreneur*. Toronto, McClelland and Stewart Limited, 1979.

Campbell, G.G. *The History of Nova Scotia*. Toronto, The Ryerson Press, 1948.

Clarke, Wayne, Judith Penner, and George Rogers. *Cruising Nova Scotia*. Toronto, Greey de Pencier Books, 1979.

Duncan, Dorothy. *Bluenose: A Portrait of Nova Scotia*. New York/London, Harper and Brothers Publishers, 1942.

Grant, George. *Joseph Howe*. Nova Scotia, A. and W. MacKinlay, 1906. (Quotes speech by Howe.)

Heritage Trust of Nova Scotia. *Founded Upon a Rock: Historic Buildings of Halifax and Vicinity Standing in 1967*. Halifax, The Heritage Trust of Nova Scotia, 1967.
– *Seasoned Timbers*, vols. 1 and 2. Halifax, The Heritage Trust of Nova Scotia, 1972, 1974.

Longley, Hon. James W. *Joseph Howe*. Toronto, Morang and Co., Ltd., 1904.

MacAskill, W.R. *Lure of the Sea*. (Introduction by Thomas H. Raddall.) Halifax, Eastern Photo Engravers, 1951.

MacDonald, H.M., ed. *The Clarsach: An Anthology of Scottish Verse*. Toronto/Montreal, The Copp Clark Co., Ltd., 1955.

Moorsom, Capt. W. *Letters from Nova Scotia*. London, Henry Colburn and Richard Bentley, 1830.

Parker, John P. *Sails of the Maritimes*. Halifax, The Maritime Museum of Canada, 1960.

Patterson, Frank H. *John Patterson: The Founder of Pictou Town*. Truro, N.S., Truro Printing and Publishing Co., Ltd., 1955.

Raddall, Thomas H. *Halifax: Warden of the North*. Toronto/Montreal, McClelland and Stewart Limited, 1971.

Teller, Walter Magnes. *The Search for Captain Slocum*. New York, Charles Scribner's Sons, 1956.

Wallace, Frederick W. *Wooden Ships and Iron Men*. London, Hodder and Stoughton, Ltd., 1924.

Witney, Dudley. *The Lighthouse*. Toronto, McClelland and Stewart Limited, 1975.

Wright, Esther Clark. *Blomidon Rose*. Toronto, The Ryerson Press, 1957.

Zim, Herbert S. and Lester Ingle. *Seashores: A Guide to Animals and Plants Along the Beaches*. New York, Golden Press, 1955.

Pamphlets

A Walking Tour of Historic Pictou. The Pictou Heritage Society. Unsigned, undated.

Haliburton House, Windsor, Nova Scotia. Halifax, Nova Scotia Museum. Unsigned, undated.

The Habitation, Port Royal National Historic Park. Ottawa, Parks Canada. Undated. IAN Publication no. QS TO76 000 BB A3.

Nova Scotia. Halifax, Nova Scotia Department of Tourism, 1981. Unsigned.

Prescott House, Starr's Point, King's County, Nova Scotia. Halifax, Nova Scotia Museum. Unsigned, undated.

Richardson, Evelyn M. *The Story of the Barrington Woolen Mill*. Barrington, N.S., Cape Sable Historical Society. Undated.

St. Paul's Church (Anglican Church of Canada), Halifax, Nova Scotia. Halifax, St Paul's Church. Unsigned, undated.

Saulnier, Janine. *St. Mary's Church and Parish*. Church Point, N.S. St Mary's Church. Undated.

Thomas McCulloch House. Halifax, Nova Scotia Museum. Undated.

Uniacke House, Mount Uniacke, Nova Scotia. Halifax, Nova Scotia Museum. Undated.

Newspaper supplement
Bruce, Harry. *Here Lies Joseph Howe*. Halifax, *The 4th Estate*, 12 April 1973.

Manuscript
Harvey, Mary Mackay. *Gardens of Shelburne, Nova Scotia, 1785-1820*. (Curatorial Report no. 27.) Halifax, Nova Scotia Museum, 1975.

Articles
Bruce, Charles. '*The Township of Time*'. *Echoes* (Imperial Order Daughters of the Empire and Children of the Empire), Autumn 1955.

Bruce, Harry. 'Keltic Lodge: Day Trips'. *Atlantic Insight Guide to Atlantic Canada*, Summer 1981.
– 'Discover Nova Scotia's Mix of History and Vitality'. *Toronto Calendar Magazine*, 28 March-1 May 1980.
– 'You Had to be Able to Build a Boat Just to Get Off the Island'. *Weekend Magazine*, 6 Oct. 1973.
– 'Claws. Sequel to Jaws?' *enRoute*, July/Aug. 1976.

Bush, Edward F. 'The Canadian Lighthouse'. *Canadian Historic Sites: Occasional Papers in Archaeology and History*, no. 9. Ottawa, Parks Canada, Indian and Northern Affairs, 1974.

Cameron, Silver Donald. 'The People of D'Escousse: Portrait of a Cape Breton Village'. *Quest*, Dec. 1981.

Stanfield, Robert. Quote used as filler in *Atlantic Insight*, Nov. 1979.

Prim Point

Millions of ferryboat passengers have seen Prim Point, cold gatepost of the Annapolis Basin. Almost four centuries ago, a gritty crew of French sailors also saw it. They were the first Europeans ever to sail in from the tidal turbulence of the Bay of Fundy, past Prim Point, and onto the smooth haven of the basin. Trees. Nothing but trees, and more trees, rimmed the water. Still, the French thought the place was 'more agreeable than any other in the world', and named it Port Royal. That was in 1604, sixteen years before the *Mayflower* landed the Pilgrims at Plymouth Rock. Shakespeare was writing *Othello*. Henry IV, first of the Bourbon kings, ruled France, and among those who made the bold voyage to the Annapolis Valley was his friend, Jean de Biencourt, Sieur de Poutrincourt, who dreamed of French settlement in North America. So was Pierre du Gua, Sieur de Monts, who dreamed of fortunes in the fur trade with Indians. And so was Captain Samuel de Champlain, who dreamed of maps, and was already making his eternal mark on the history of exploration. In time, many more French would sail past Prim Point, and, fulfilling Poutrincourt's dream, they would sink roots in the Annapolis Valley. They would build a culture of survival.

Brier Island (left)

On Brier Island, Nova Scotian writer Will R. Bird said in 1956, basalt cliffs form 'a striking assemblage of regular columnar masses which sometimes descend in continuous ranges of steps for hundreds of yards into the sea. Serrated ridges, rising here and there above the surface of the water, appear at first sight like so much pierwork reared in defence of the island.' The most powerful tides in the world ceaselessly abuse Brier Island – it's the western extremity of Digby Neck in the Bay of Fundy – and it's beloved not only by bird-watchers and agate-hunters but also by yachtsmen who revere the memory of Captain Joshua Slocum. He spent his boyhood here, ran away to sea, and began the singular career that culminated in his becoming the first man ever to sail around the world alone. That was back in the 1890s. If Slocum were alive today, he'd recognize the island of his boyhood. It hasn't changed all that much. Now, as ever, its strange rocks endure their regular beatings from the sea.

Rocks, Sandy Cove

Just for a moment, the low sun heats grainy rock at Sandy Cove, Digby Neck. There are other sandy coves in Nova Scotia, not to mention Sand Beach, Sand Point, Sand River, and Sandy Point, but these places cannot boast of an unsolved mystery about a legless foreigner. It was on this beach, the Sandy Cove beach, that in the summer of 1863 two fishermen found a helpless, moaning stranger with a jug of water and a loaf of black bread. He had recently lost both his legs above the knees. The amputations were the work of an unknown doctor and, though a strange vessel had been seen tacking just offshore the evening before, no one knew who had dumped this agonized character on the people of Sandy Cove. Since he spoke no English, they took him down St Mary's Bay to Nova Scotia's 'French Shore'. There, folks named him 'Jerome' and looked after him for forty years. Since he rarely talked in any language, they never did discover his birthplace, how he'd lost his legs, or how he'd arrived among them like a piece of flotsam. He took his secret to his grave, and at Sandy Cove the rocks aren't talking.

Cabot Trail, North Shore

Old mountains meet an older sea on the Cabot Trail. The most beloved territory of Alexander Graham Bell (1847-1922) was neither Edinburgh, his birthplace; nor Brantford, Ont., where he conceived the telephone in 1874; nor Boston, where his phone was born in 1875. No, it was his summer estate at *Beinn Bhreagh* (Gaelic for 'beautiful mountain') in Baddeck, Cape Breton Island, Nova Scotia. Baddeck is the beginning and end of the circular, spectacular, and mostly coastal highway known as the Cabot Trail. 'I have travelled around the globe,' Bell wrote. 'I have seen the Canadian Rockies, the Andes and the Highlands of Scotland. But for simple beauty, Cape Breton outrivals them all.'

On the Cabot Trail

The Cabot Trail is 184 miles of roaring seascapes, white bluffs, lush glens, and windy, bird's-eye views of ocean, forest, and stone. Both its breath-catching physical drama and its human heritage echo in its place-names: Indian Brook, Cheticamp, Skir Dhu, Briton Cove, Wreck Cove, Cape North, Cape Smoky, Sugar Loaf, Cap Rouge, Jumping Brook Valley, Mackenzie and French mountains.... Cape Breton's French-speaking Acadian settlers and Gaelic-speaking Scottish settlers were both dispossessed peoples with long memories; and one of Canada's more enduring expressions of racial homesickness is the Cabot Trail's 'Lone Shieling'. It's a stone replica of a Scottish crofter's hut. There, a plaque offers mournful lines from *The Canadian Boat Song*:

From the lone shieling of the misty island
Mountains divide us, and the waste of seas —
Yet still the blood is strong, the heart is highland
And we in dreams behold the Hebrides.

Old house, Freeport

Freeport's pretty far down Digby Neck. You take a car-ferry to get there, and if you're heading even further west, to Brier Island, you'll take another ferry across a tidal raceway. Freeport, in short, is not a place where you need worry much about urban blight. It used to be Long Island, but an Act of Parliament changed its name. That was just a while back, in 1865. The population's nudging 500 these days. Freeport's a good spot for deep-sea fishing. A fellow named Alec McGovern once wrote some verse about the village. Maybe he was sitting outside a sea-weathered door when he wrote it. Anyway, after inviting the reader to

'Come down to fog-bound Freeport at the end of dear knows where,' he continued:

This is the lair of the restless sea where the waves
come down to rest,
After they've curled over half the world in their
infinite rolling quest.
This is the land of the simple heart (that you dream
of now and then),
Where there's no demand in the outstretched hand,
and eyes are the eyes of men.

Mill stone, Fort Anne

The mill stone – at Fort Anne, near Annapolis Royal – is one of the first that Europeans used in North America. According to one story, it was only after the terrible exertion of grinding corn by hand had killed six men that the French built the continent's first grist mill. It rose just south of what is now Annapolis Royal in the first decade of the 1600s, and it was soon so important that the French built a primitive battery to protect it. This was Fort Anne. If some wives are house-proud, Annapolis Royal is history-proud. Its people happily recite its 'firsts', and, though the British drove the French out more than two centuries ago, the firsts are almost all French firsts: the first permanent white settlement in North America (1605), the first social club and gourmet society (the Order of Good Cheer, 1606), the first drama productions, the first sowing of grain and planting of trees by Europeans, the first brick factory, iron mine, baptism, ship-building, road-making, and so on. Fort Anne, the first national historic park in Canada (1917), was once 'the football of the nations'. French and English bloodily wrested it from each other no fewer than seven times, but, these days, it's peaceful enough. Each summer, it attracts 130,000 visitors.

L'Habitation

Nine miles from Annapolis Royal, on the north shore of the Annapolis Basin, lies Port Royal National Park and a replica of *l'Habitation*. It's as close as you'll ever get to knowing about life in the earliest permanent white settlement north of the Gulf of Mexico. Geographer and explorer Samuel de Champlain was still only thirty-five when, in 1605, he drew up plans for *l'Habitation* and, along with fur-trader François Du Pont-Gravé, supervised its construction. It was like a sixteenth-century Normandy farm, in which buildings surrounded a square courtyard.

The colonists included Catholic priests and Huguenot ministers, criminals and noblemen, as well as a useful assortment of shipwrights, masons, blacksmiths, and armourers. Champlain went on from there. He built another settlement at Quebec in 1608, and eventually became 'the father of New France'. Back in the Annapolis Valley, *l'Habitation* became a foundation for a century or more of French Acadian dyke-building, fruit-growing, and cattle-raising.

Annapolis Royal

Twice in 1707, Governor Daniel Auger de Subercase fought off fierce raids by New Englanders on Port Royal. In 1710, he wrote a frantic letter to France: 'If we do not receive help, I have every reason to dread something disastrous....All are in despair, for they look in vain for supplies they badly need...and the harvest has been poor....Besides, I have no money....I have paid all that I can raise by selling all my possessions. I am ready to give even my shirt....My trouble will be for nothing if we do not receive help.' Help never came. Instead, a few days later, the New Englanders and British were back – with a bigger, more determined force. Though they outnumbered the French seven to one, it took them eight days to take Port Royal. Subercase, swashbuckling even in defeat, told them, 'I deliver to you the keys of the fort, in the hope of paying you a visit next Spring.' He never returned. In 1713, the Treaty of Utrecht ceded part of Acadia to Britain. The part became Nova Scotia.

Annapolis Royal

A generation of peace followed the treaty, and Acadian farmers flourished in the Annapolis Valley. They raised big families and big crops. But Port Royal languished. It didn't greatly interest its new Mother Country. The British changed its name to Annapolis Royal and, until 1749, let it remain the capital of Nova Scotia. Then they built a new capital, and called it Halifax. Now, Annapolis Royal was just a garrison town, a pretty backwater that dozed in the sun at the western end of a magical valley. It stayed that way for generation after generation. That's the secret of its ghostly charm today.

12

Longfellow, Grand Pré

When relations between France and Britain returned to normal, which meant bloody, the British decided they could not trust the Acadians; and on 5 September 1755, at the church of St Charles, Grand Pré, hundreds of Acadians heard harsh words from Governor Charles Lawrence: 'That your lands and tenements, cattle of all kinds and livestock of all sorts, are forfeited to the Crown, and you yourself to be removed from this....Province.' Thus began the saddest exodus in Canadian history, the departure of the Acadians for France, the Thirteen Colonies, the Magdalen Islands, anywhere that seemed to promise survival. More than ninety years later, Henry Wadsworth Longfellow, an American who had never seen the Annapolis Valley, wrote his dolorous poem, *Evange-*

line: a Tale of Acadie. It was about two lovers, separated by the expulsion, and it struck nineteenth-century readers as exquisitely sad. It became a kind of *Gone With the Wind* of the age of narrative verse, and, long after the poet's death in 1882, Nova Scotia continued to beat tourism drums about 'the far-famed Land of Evangeline'. Now, Grand Pré National Historic Park boasts a replica of St Charles church; a graceful bronze statue of the mythical Evangeline; and a white bust of the poet who unwittingly did so much for the travel business in Nova Scotia. 'This is the forest primeval,' reads the opening line of *Evangeline*. Grand Pré is scarcely a forest primeval these days, but then again it wasn't at the time of the expulsion either. Acadians had been farming the valley for more than a century.

First Acadian cemetery

Slowly and bravely, exiles returned. In 1763, the Treaty of Paris gave to Britain both Quebec and what was left of Acadia. Victorious Britain no longer feared Acadians, and in 1768 hundreds made a pilgrimage from Massachusetts, through Maine and New Brunswick, back to the Annapolis Valley. They found their houses gone, and strangers on their land. Puritan planters from New England – remembered in later Annapolis Valley verse as 'the junior Pilgrim fathers' – had gobbled up the choice farms Britain had forced the Acadians to abandon. So the Acadians hiked right through the valley to the western end of Nova Scotia where, despite the expulsion, some of their people were carving out a living. They settled on St Mary's Bay, proved fine farmers could become fine fishermen,

eventually built villages that merged so seamlessly they turned the coastal road into what one writer has called 'The longest main street in America'. Grosse Coques is among those villages. It boasts a graveyard with a marker in memory of Marie Doucet, dated 1771; and a frame house with a plaque that declares its date of construction as 1768, 'the year the township [of Clare] was established for the Acadians who had remained in the province after 1755 and for those who had wandered back from exile.' Grosse Coques, incidentally, means 'big clams'. Without big clams, the story goes, the first Acadians on this shore might never have survived the winters. The clams are meaty still, just as they were when Marie Doucet was laid to rest.

Covenanter Church

'Its plain walls tell of the severe and sturdy faith which used to be thundered down from its heavy pulpit upon its pew boxes,' British Prime Minister Ramsay MacDonald wrote after a visit to Nova Scotia. 'How heavily laden with the sins of their neighbours must the preachers have been whose feet wore those deep hollows in its pulpit steps.' MacDonald was describing the Covenanter Church at Grand Pré in the Annapolis Valley. Among the New Englanders and Britishers who replaced the Roman Catholic Acadians, there were both Congregationalists and stern spiritual heirs of the Solemn League and Cove-

nant that in 1643 had established the Presbyterian faith in England and Scotland. In Grand Pré, in 1790, they helped found North America's first agricultural society, and its motto tightly expressed their outlook on life: 'Be industrious that you may live.' With pine, spruce, wooden pins, hand-hewn timbers and hand-made nails, they industriously raised the Covenanter Church. They finished it in 1811, and added the tower and spire in 1818. It's part of the United Church of Canada now. Its double pulpit still rises half-way to the ceiling, and maybe a distance towards heaven.

Citadel, Clock Tower

The Old Town Clock in Halifax is like the Eiffel Tower, the Tower of London, the Empire State Building or, on a more appropriate scale, the little bronze mermaid in the harbour at Copenhagen. It's the symbol of a city. From 1794 to 1800, the Commander-in-Chief of Nova Scotia was no less a figure than Edward, Duke of Kent, future father of Queen Victoria. He was an austere, athletic, intelligent, soldierly prince with a passion both for his French mistress and for toys and punctuality. Wherever he travelled, Nova Scotian author Thomas Raddall wrote, 'His quarters were cluttered with music boxes, artificial singing birds, toy organs with dancing horses, and watches and clocks of all kinds, especially those that rang chimes or played a tune.' The prince thought both soldiers and civilians in Halifax badly needed a chiming garrison clock, and he ordered his engineers to design one. 'It was installed in 1803,' Raddall wrote, 'and remains the chief memento of the royal martinet and perhaps the best-known feature of the city.'

Dalhousie University (right)

A weathervane confronts the salty grey sky above Dalhousie University in Halifax, and its profile trumpets history. The ninth Earl of Dalhousie founded the university in 1818 (though it didn't formally open till 1843), and the vane sports his family crest. He launched Dalhousie with revenue the British had siphoned out of Maine. Troops from Halifax had captured eastern Maine in the War of 1812, and the customs duties they collected there amounted to a tidy sum for the founding of a university. So Lieutenant-Governor Dalhousie founded one; and, rare in its time, it welcomed students of all faiths. It remains today, as Thomas Raddall put it, 'A monument to the wisdom of the Scottish nobleman, not only in its many fine buildings but in the long list of Nova Scotians and others who have found wisdom within its walls.' Worse causes have swallowed up the spoils of war.

18

Quilt and 'Deutsche' Church, Brunswick Street

W hen Governor Edward Cornwallis founded Halifax – the fortress city that Rudyard Kipling would one day call 'the Warden of the Honour of the North' – he brought with him a mob of cockney settlers. Low-life from London slums, they were disastrously unsuitable pioneers, and in that first Halifax winter (1749-50) typhus slaughtered hundreds. Cornwallis now sought tougher, cleaner, more industrious settlers, and he got them. Most were Rhineland Germans, some were French Protestants, a few were Swiss. Since the Germans called themselves 'Deutsche', English-speaking Halifax lumped them all together as 'Dutch'. That's why Haligonians still call the first Lutheran church in Canada 'the old Dutch church', or sometimes 'the little Dutch church'. It stands on Brunswick street in north-end Halifax (and also at the right end of the centre row of a hand-crafted quilt). It may never have been Dutch but it's certainly old and it's certainly little. The Germans built it in 1756, and it's just forty feet long by twenty wide.

St John's Anglican Church, Lunenburg

If Rome wasn't built in a day, neither was St John's Anglican Church, Lunenburg. Jean Baptiste Moreau, a Huguenot, preached outdoors to the German, French, and Swiss settlers all through the summer of 1753. On 4 October 1754, he wrote that 'The church, 40 by 60 feet, was nearly finished.' But the following spring, construction was still under way, and Governor Charles Lawrence reported that he'd heard the carpenter had been 'too lavish in ornamenting the building.' Five years later, it still wasn't finished. Services did occur there, but the church let in so much snow and rain that, in bad weather, the congregation fled. By 1763, a decade after Moreau's outdoor sermons, Rev. Robert Vincent assured the Society for the Propagation of the Gospel that, if he could get 259 pounds sterling to complete the job, 'the church will then be neat and commodious.' The money would also finance construction of a palisade round the church to protect Lunenburgers during raids. It took another seventy-nine years–till 1842–to finish the bell tower, though the present tower is merely 108 years old. St John's was founded by royal charter. King George III presented its communion vessels, and visitors may still view its Queen Anne chalice, made of pewter. More than once during the past couple of centuries, hard times have almost closed St John's; but, like Lunenburg itself, it has proved to be a survivor.

St George's Church, Halifax

St George's Church, also known as 'the Round Church', is one of four Halifax structures that stand today because, 180-odd years ago, a British prince had a curious love of the circular. Edward, Duke of Kent (see page 16), also commissioned the round Music Room at Prince's Lodge on Bedford Basin, the round Town Clock on Citadel Hill, and the round Martello Tower in Point Pleasant Park. Sir John Wentworth, Lieutenant-Governor, laid the cornerstone for St George's on 10 April 1800; and the Right Reverend John Inglis, third bishop of Nova Scotia, consecrated the church. Halley's comet flashed into sight in 1835, and so impressed the rector of St George's that he mounted a comet-shaped weathervane on the cupola. In the church's earliest days, the bone-bruising upper galleries were reserved for soldiers, servants and slaves. By 1841 St George's was so popular that it enlarged its seating capacity and, 141 years later, it remains one of the most beloved churches in Halifax. Despite its location in a downtown neighbourhood that has seen generations of buildings rise and fall, St George's continues to defy the wrecker's ball.

22

Royal Pew, St Paul's Church

The Royal Pew at St Paul's Anglican Church glows with rich tradition and declares that this, the oldest building in Halifax and the first Protestant house of God in Canada, is a church of royal foundation. The Crown imported its oak frames and pine timbers from Boston and Portsmouth, New Hampshire; and on Sunday, 2 September 1750, only one year after the city was founded, St Paul's opened its doors to worshippers for the first time. It was 'the mother temple of the Church of England in Canada', the first Anglican cathedral among all the British colonies, the first garrison church in Canada. It lays claim, with a touch of grandiosity, to the title, 'the Westminster Abbey of Canada'. No building exudes more Halifax history. As decades became generations and generations became centuries, various additions, renovations, adjustments, and embellishments kept changing St Paul's, but its grip on Halifax emotions remained constant. On 24 October 1857, the Acadian *Recorder* exulted over a shingling job: 'Who shall say after this that Halifax is a mean-looking place; that the people have no taste for architecture; that the wealthiest congregation in the Province worships God in the most disreputable-looking temple? Let those who have long been making such remarks...now close their mouths forever....Let the architects of the renaissance clap their hands with joy. Let everybody's grandmother

feel young again. St Paul's Church, that glorious, old, wooden, loggen pile of the tea-chest order, whom some barbarians have wished for years to see sold for fuel and replaced by an awful gothic edifice in stone...that dear, moldy, dingy, musty, rotten, dirty, lovely old St Paul's is to be propped up a while longer. It is actually getting a new coat of shingles.' That 'while longer' has stretched to 125 years.

St Paul's Church

A bluenose poet named Arthur Wentworth Eaton once celebrated the durability of St Paul's in this fashion:
Timbered in times when men built strong;
With a tower of wood grown grey,
The frame of it old, the heart still young,
It has stood for many a day.

A bronze memorial arch, a tribute to those among the congregation who fell in the First World War, frames the entrance to the nave, and a church publication recommends that 'you begin your tour' by standing under the arch and looking up the main aisle. 'The effect is one of spaciousness, antiquity and beauty. St Paul's has five aisles, a feature it shares with only six other Anglican Churches in the world – all of them in England and Scotland.' And none of them wooden.

Church built in a day

Few small cities honour their dead more conspicuously than Halifax. This is partly accidental. Like weeds crowding a garden, the city has grown up in a haphazard fashion all around the green, grey, orderly burial grounds of long-gone victims of shipwrecks, waterfront murders, dreadful epidemics, explosions, warfare, and, among the lucky, simple age. Holy Cross is one such cemetery. Its graves include those of two sailors hanged for piracy in 1844 and, on the higher end of the social scale, that of Sir John Sparrow David Thompson. One of Canada's least famous prime ministers, he died at Windsor Castle in 1894 while a guest of Queen Victoria. Holy Cross Cemetery also contains the chapel of Our Lady of Sorrows. The chapel has wooden carvings from a Flemish church of the 1550s, and a stained-glass window that dates back to 1661. What's most memorable about it, however, is that the people of St Mary's Parish got together and built it in one day. Only God knows exactly how many had a hand in its construction. All *we* know is that they started and finished on 31 August 1843; and that, ever since, the chapel has been a comfort to those in sorrow.

Pioneer Baptist pewter communion service

'In the service of the Church,' G.G. Campbell wrote in *The History of Nova Scotia*, the pioneers 'found something of the beauty and emotional appeal which the hardness of their lives denied to them elsewhere.' Beauty glowed from such treasures of ceremony as this pewter communion service, gift of Cedar Lake United Baptist Church to the Yarmouth County Museum. Once the property of the Free Will Baptist Church, which was built around 1840 at Beaver River, the pewter had probably come to Yarmouth County from New England decades earlier. It may even have been in the county during Henry Alline's short, charismatic career as a preacher (1776-83). In *The Neutral Yankees of Nova Scotia* (1937), John Bartlet Brebner described Alline as 'a saintly, tubercular, young evangelist from Falmouth [N.S.] whose self-elected task it was to combat all creeds save his own while visiting practically all of the settlements to snatch complacent brands from the burning....But, gifted with an extraordinary religious eloquence and driven on by God's commands, he toured all the settlements of Nova Scotia and shattered their congregations, leaving his converts filled with consuming moral zeal but without an orderly structure.' After his death, most of his followers gradually formed the Baptist Church of Nova Scotia.

Kilmarnock House, Pictou

Kilmarnock House, Water Street, Pictou, is a stone throwback to a period when Pictou was the first port-of-call for tens of thousands of Scots who'd abandoned their homeland to make new lives in a new world. In its early days, Pictou was a thriving, brawling lumber port, a place where Royal Navy press gangs kidnapped farmers for sea duty, a place of drunken sailors, drunken disbanded soldiers, drunken sons of affluent merchants, muggers, and rum dives, that offered whatever was needed to ignite violence. It was also a town of harsh Presbyterianism, in which church elders relied on such tools of justice as the whipping post, the branding iron, the pillory, and the rope. By the time Kilmarnock House was built (around 1825), Pictou had begun to settle down. Violence was no longer habitual. Merchants worried about lumber, fish, mort-gages, and accounts six days a week, and about Heaven and Hell on the seventh. Kilmarnock House was their kind of building: Scottish, sturdy, stone, with five-sided dormer windows. It served as a bank for a while and, more recently, as a gift shop. It's not far from the waterfront, and in Pictou that's always been the scene of the action.

McCulloch House, Pictou

McCulloch House, Pictou, was the home of the most able of all the able Scots who flocked to Nova Scotia in the early 1800s. The Reverend Thomas McCulloch arrived in Pictou in 1803 with a wife, children, and a pile of books. He preached, he taught, he cared for the sick. He founded a school. The day-to-day rulers of Nova Scotia lived in Halifax. They were colonial versions of English aristocrats, and their school, King's College, granted degrees only to adherents of the Church of England. Presbyterians, of no matter what stripe, need not have applied. The powerful Halifax compact was disinclined to spend public money on a college for trouble-making Scots in a distant and primitive county. McCulloch's stubborn campaign for Pictou Academy therefore became not only an underdogs' fight for the right to state-supported educa-

tion for their children, but also part of the whole seething battle for responsible government in the British colonies. He won and, as author Dorothy Duncan explained in the next century, the Academy eventually graduated 'eight university presidents, two premiers, two governors, four judges, and hundreds of teachers, clergymen, professors, lawyers and doctors.' To build his house in 1806, McCulloch used bricks from Scotland. J.J. Audubon, king of naturalist-painters, visited him here in 1833 and said that McCulloch's mounted birds were the finest private collection in North America. But McCulloch sold a lot of the birds at London auctions. Often, the Academy was strapped for money, and he'd do just about anything to keep that school going.

Ross Farm, New Ross

The Ross Farm Museum of Agriculture, 15 miles north of Chester in Lunenburg County, boasts a farmhouse built in 1817, a barn built in 1892, and an exhibit of ancient farm equipment, all of which is what you'd expect. But it also breathes, smells, makes noises, produces food, and lives by the seasons. Oxen go about their old jobs here. Men and women work and sweat here. They shear sheep, flail grain, press cider, make barrels and sauerkraut. If Ross Farm is an educational experiment today, it was also an experiment at its birth in 1816. The governor then, the Earl of Dalhousie, asked Captain William Ross to take 172 discharged Nova Scotia Fencibles and found a settlement somewhere between the Atlantic coast and the Annapolis Valley. All did not go well. As a county historian once put it, 'The disbanded troops were amply provided with ration biscuit, ration beef, and ration port, while ration rum, arriving in puncheons, kept their spirits from flagging. The number was increased by soldiers of the German Legion who had seen active service under Napoleon, by some of the Newfoundland Fencibles, and a few of the Fourteenth Foot. As long as rations continued to arrive it was "high day and holiday, and bonfire night." After three years, "some left in disgust...sold for a trifle, or deserted their claims." ' But Ross stayed, and in 1819 got his reward: a grant of 800 acres. Others got smaller grants, and the colonial government, to help families get started, also provided tools, seed, bake ovens, rope, twine, wax, thread. It was a hard life but some endured; and, today, Ross Farm shows how.

Meeting House, Barrington

Nothing in this lucid summer day suggests the grimness of bygone gatherings in the white frame building. For this was the Meeting House, Barrington, N.S. Barrington was once a French village (La Passage), but in 1755 New Englanders burned the town, slaughtered its livestock, and carried the French off to Boston. Soon, settlers from Massachusetts arrived. They included Nonconformists–rabid Puritan fundamentalists–who began to build the Meeting House in 1765, and even before it had doors, windows, or seats, held their first service in it. 'Religion was a stern affair,' G.G. Campbell wrote in *The History of Nova Scotia* (1948). 'Dancing and card-playing were condemned. Heads of families who did not attend church were fined, and the young person who smiled in a meeting, if she escaped a public rebuke from the minister . . . would receive more painful punishment at the hands of her father.' The people were poor. Men could work on the church only in the time between fishing and farming. Gospel sessions were long, and often cold. It wasn't till the 1780s or 1790s that the hall had doors and windows, and church records don't mention such luxuries as firewood and candles till 1841. The Meeting House was both church and town hall; but in 1838 some insisted on separating church and state. Records reveal that 'The Town meeting was held on the earth by the side of the Old Meeting House (the doors of which having been shut against the Town).' Today, the oldest Nonconformist church in Canada is a museum, and the sun is shining.

Sackville Manor House (Tolson House) (left)

Gateposts at Sackville Manor House, Bedford, just north of Halifax, once sailed the seas. They're pieces of ribs from the *Charybdis*, which some call 'the first Canadian warship'. Built in Chatham, England, in 1859, and assigned to Halifax by the Royal Navy, she was a 200-foot-long, 2,250-ton wooden corvette, driven by both steam and sail. After she'd done her duty and been broken up, pieces of her ribs somehow ended up as ornaments at the entrance to the Manor House estate. The house itself is much older than the gateposts. Joseph Scott, a sawmill-operator, ex-military man, and local judge, built it, probably in 1771. Surrounded by urban sprawl these days, the house once stood in lonely splendour on the only road from Halifax to the heart of Nova Scotia. Important northbound people stopped there regularly. Fleet surgeon John Ternan bought the house in 1872, and it remained in his family till 1946. After that the Tolson family lovingly restored it. Tolsons have lived there ever since. Aside from the sea-going gateposts, it boasts original beams of Norwegian oak, a gambrel roof, and unusual wish-bone chimneys.

Martock House, Windsor

The style and face of Martock House, which preens itself on a mound near Windsor, have changed like those of a fashion-conscious woman who just happens to have lived for a century or two. John Butler, a British-born Halifax merchant and a member of the tight compact that ruled Nova Scotia in the late 1700s, got the site as part of a large land grant after the expulsion of the Acadians. He built a sturdy summer house there, and named it after his home in Somerset. He bequeathed the place to his nephew, John Butler Dight, on condition that Dight change his surname to Butler. The new owner, now John D. Butler, became commissary to the Duke of Wellington's army in the Peninsular war; and his son, Edward Kent Strathlorne Butler, rose to the rank of colonel of the 35th Royal Sussex Regiment. The younger Butler retired in 1839, and moved in with his father at Martock House. It was the colonel who changed the unpretentious two-storey dwelling into something that looked as though it belonged in the American South. He added wings with their own columns. He built the hefty portico and supported it with bigger columns, each made from a local tree trunk, each topped with an Ionic capital. The house has an impressive circular stairway, and a history of physical change, inside and out. Owners have removed and added wings, altered doorways, lowered the roof. The colonel died in 1871, and since that was also the year in which fire consumed King's College School, Martock served as a schoolhouse for a while. In our time, the owner has been Ernest E. Sweet. (In another time, his grandfather was a tenant farmer on the same estate.) It's to Sweet's credit that the Greek Revival façade, the old colonel's most extravagant indulgence, still outfaces a decidedly un-Greek climate.

Uniacke House

Uniacke House, the way it was. A public museum now, this remarkable mansion is a monument to a remarkable red-headed Irishman. Born in 1753 to a landed family in County Cork, Richard John Uniacke was disinherited after a violent quarrel with his father. He arrived in Philadelphia in 1774, met Moses Delesdernier, became his assistant land agent at Fort Cumberland, N.B., and married his twelve-year-old daughter. In 1776, when Uniacke was twenty-three, he joined an attack on the fort by Yankee rebels, was captured, and taken under guard to Halifax. During the trip, between Windsor and Halifax, he saw land that reminded him of the family estate he'd lost forever. In time, he'd own 5,000 acres of that land. He'd put a mansion of his own on it, and a coach-house, greenhouse, barns, imported cattle, and cottages for his workers. Meanwhile, his flirtation with the Yankees could not stop his astonishing rise as a lawyer and civil servant. By 1781, he was Solicitor-General for Nova Scotia. By 1789, he was

Speaker of the House of Assembly. By 1797 he was Attor-
ney-General. When England seemed constantly at war he
served, too, as Advocate-General in the Nova Scotia Vice-
Admiralty Court. Uniacke revised the laws of the province,
got rich, and fathered twelve children. After his child bride
died in 1803, he married the daughter of a British army
officer, and she bore him a thirteenth child. He served on
the Legislative Council, Nova Scotia's upper house, till he
died in 1830. He was seventy-seven, and he'd been enjoy-
ing Mount Uniacke ever since he'd finished the house in
1815. 'For fifteen years,' Annapolis Valley author Esther C.
Wright wrote, 'Richard Uniacke sat at the head of the great
mahogany table, which still stands in the diningroom, read
the books which still fill the shelves in the library, read
morning prayers beside the wood stove, which still stands
in the hall, to servants, who sat in the twelve Adam chairs,
which still line the stairway.'

Leaves of borage

Leaves of borage, like mint, make a cool summer drink, and the flowers are edible both in salads and as candied cake decorations. Early Nova Scotians used both wild and cultivated plants not only for cooking but also for medicine. To cure conditions as severe as breast cancer or as harmless as baldness, as grim as scurvy, dysentery, or 'raging madness' or as mild as chapped hands, heartburn, or blood-shot eyes, settlers had little choice but to rely on the ancient herbal remedies that their forebears had known in Britain. Their medicinal concoctions consisted of powders, poultices, salves, juices, and syrups, made from blossoms, leaves, grasses, roots, buds, berries, and barks. Often, the formula also called for unsavoury parts of animals and reptiles, ground up or dried out. Sometimes the remedies worked. Sometimes they failed. For Mrs William Booth, who lived in Shelburne in the 1780s, they failed. In 1975 Mary Mackay Harvey, a curatorial assistant with the Nova Scotia Museum, revealed Mrs Booth's fate: 'While [Captain] Booth was in Shelburne his wife Hannah became ill and he describes the herbal remedies prescribed for her, such as cream of tartar in water, and wine with sugar; peppermint water and chammomile tea. Her body was rubbed with flowers of the mustard when she had pains and spasms. During the last stages of her illness, she suffered severe fever and was given a poultice of mustard and vinegar. She died, whether as a result of the remedies or the sickness is not clear.'

Prescott House, Acacia Grove

Prescott House, which overlooks the serpentine Cornwallis River at Starr's Point, was the chosen head-quarters of a Halifax-born businessman who helped turn the Annapolis-Cornwallis Valley into 'the apple orchard of the British Empire'. Charles Ramage Prescott (1772-1859) retired from business while still young and, for his health's sake, left Halifax. The valley was drier and sunnier (and still is). He called his 100-acre farm Acacia Grove. There, he turned his attention to horticulture, and particularly to apples. From Britain, he imported Gravensteins, Ribstons, Blenheims, Alexanders, Golden Pippins. From the United States and Quebec, he brought in other varieties. He tried new kinds of wheat, nut trees, pear trees, grapes; and he offered 'scions and buds of any kind to every person who may apply in the proper season.' Acacia Grove, in Charles Prescott's time, hummed with parties, berry-picking forays, and farming experiments. Mud from the Cornwallis River provided the bricks for his twenty-one-room mansion. The estate raised purebreed cattle, sheep, horses, and fifty varieties of roses. The valley, it turned out, was indeed good for Prescott's health. He didn't die till he was eighty-seven. After that, the property had a string of owners. It deteriorated; somebody cut down the acacia trees, and, for a time, the mansion was a bunkhouse for itinerant farm labourers. But in 1942, Prescott's great-granddaughter, Mary Allison Prescott, bought and restored the house, and she and her sisters moved in. The Nova Scotia government bought it after her death, and it's now a museum.

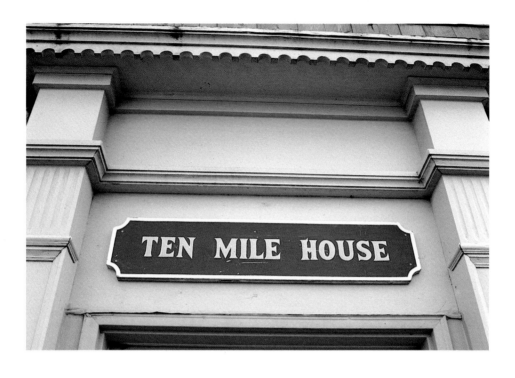

Ten Mile House, Bedford

Ten Mile House, ten miles north of Halifax, has done duty in this century as a hotel, rooming-house, art gallery, and antique shop, but in its boisterous heyday it was a stage-coach inn. It's a wooden two-and-half storey building in the Georgian style, and has six fireplaces. Joseph Scott (see Manor House gateposts, page 30), an army officer who'd served with General James Wolfe at the taking of Quebec in 1759, built it in 1790. Later, it had a series of owners, including a man with twenty children whose appropriate name was Increase Ward. Captain W. Moorsom, an Englishman, described Nova Scotia inns in 1830: 'The last crack of the whip which in England, places, as if by magic, a stable boy at the head of each leader and a waiter at the door, here dies away unheeded in an echo among the woods. . . . Yet I confess myself a great admirer of these little inns. There is a style of simplicity [and] a few fair words aptly employed will ensure an attention and good-will far beyond those of more splendid establishments.' Parties from Halifax, including hundreds of men in horse-drawn sleighs, sometimes fueled up on hot spiced port, then charged up to Ten Mile House and onward to Fultz's Twelve Mile House, arriving for dinner at three p.m. With claret, port, sherry and madeira, 'dinner' lasted six hours. Then the merry bugle sounded and, with curses and laughter breaking the frosty air, with bells jingling and sleighs colliding, the roisterers all tried to head home. The horses knew the way.

Temperance Hall, Sherbrooke Village

The Temperance Hall, Sherbrooke Village, was like dozens of others that sprang up all over Nova Scotia to combat the demon rum. A small gold rush caused an economic boom in Sherbrooke in the 1860s, and brought with it so much booze that the citizens urged the House of Assembly to do something about 'parties engaged in the traffic in ardent spirits.... Enough has occurred within a few weeks to alarm those who have the best interests of the Community at heart.' The churches and all respectable womankind in Nova Scotia fought liquor ceaselessly, and children grew up amid the battle's din. For many, the social event of the week was the meeting of the temperance society. There, they'd play games, flirt, pray, and fight booze. On 10 June 1906, *The Maritime Baptist* – which believed the bar-room door was 'A bar to heaven, a door to hell/ Whoever named it, named it well' – published a letter that summed up many a good bluenose woman's attitude toward drink. It was an eloquent call to arms for legislative war on the liquor trade: 'I see that cursed, hydra-headed monster of intemperance writhing its sinuous form through our country, rearing itself aloft in every village, and thrusting its very head at our doors, and hissing in our faces, as if it knew security.... Men of Canada! Christian voters! It is time you threw away all selfish motives and asserted your manhood, realizing that only a short time hence the most you will need will be your "Body breadth in a six-foot grave".'

Eyebrow window, Lanz Street, Halifax

Hinges, Haliburton House

Hinges at Haliburton House, in Windsor, are unions of the letters 'H' and 'L', standing for 'Holy Lord'. New Englanders used them in the early 1700s to repel the powers of witchcraft and, more than a century later, their good magic must still have appealed to Nova Scotia's most renowned author. When Thomas Chandler Haliburton built the fifteen-room mansion that he called Clifton, in 1836, he made sure it had not only skylights, huge fire-places and ovens, a vaulted ceiling in the dining room, and a graceful staircase in the hall, but also Holy Lord hinges. They seem to have worked. They kept the witches away long enough to enable Haliburton to continue his writing about Sam Slick, a fast-talking Yankee clock-pedlar who, while dispersing wisecracks about human nature, exploited the pomposity, venality, and gullibility of his bluenose customers. British and American readers thought Haliburton was a comic genius. Nova Scotians weren't so sure, even after the *Illustrated London News* decided he combined 'the qualities of English and Scotch humour: the hearty, mellow spirit of the one, and the shrewd, caustic qualities of the other.' Haliburton's Sam Slick tales ran to more than fifty editions. The Nova Scotia Museum runs Clifton now. It offers a chance to see how an affluent Nova Scotian gent lived in the middle of the last century, and the room where he created not only Sam Slick but also expressions that remain familiar to everyone who speaks English: 'raining cats and dogs'…'quick as a wink'…'barking up the wrong tree'…'jack of all trades and master of none'…'an ounce of prevention is worth a pound of cure'.

St Mary's Church, French Shore (left)

Whatever one thinks of its design, St Mary's Church (1905) was a mighty achievement for the French Shore. It's still the biggest wooden church in Canada and, though superlatives are hard to prove, surely it's also among the biggest wooden churches in the world. As its fairy-tale profile shoots towards heaven, St Mary's dominates the village of Church Point. The village population nudges 300; the church seats 750. Each of the twelve pillars that support its soaring arches was once a tree from a parishioner's woodlot. The steeple rises 185 feet, contains bronze bells that weigh 3,740 pounds. Another big fact about Church Point is the Université Sainte Anne, founded in 1891 by priests from France. Acadian youngsters do not feel out of place at Sainte Anne's. There's a memorial to Abbé Sigogne on campus. A saintly fugitive from the French Revolution, he settled on the shores of St Mary's Bay in 1799 and did good works among the Acadians for almost half a century. In 1830 Captain W. Moorsom wrote, 'He is at once the priest, the lawyer, and the judge of his people; he has seen most of them rise up to manhood around him. . . . The unvarying steadiness of his conduct has gained equally their affection and respect.'

St Bernard, French Shore

It was faith in God that gave the Acadians the strength and equanimity to endure the gruelling hike from the United States back to Nova Scotia, a harder life on the French Shore than they'd once known in the Annapolis Valley, and the fact of death. This graveyard is at St Bernard (population: 324). The nearby church is a massive stone affair that seats 1,000. It was made with huge blocks of granite brought from Shelburne by rail, then hauled by oxen to the church site. Construction began in 1910, but to avoid debt, the people built it a little at a time. They didn't finish till 1942. If history had taught the Acadians anything it was patience. The French Shore runs for forty miles along St Mary's Bay, Digby County. It includes the township of Clare, which the colonial government set aside in 1768 for Acadians who'd been expelled but wanted to return. 'In practical traits of social morality,' Captain Moorsom wrote, 'they shine pre-eminent. Their community. . .is like a large family. Should one of their members be left a widow without any immediate protector or means of support, her neighbours unite their labours in tilling her land, securing the crops and cutting her winter fuel. Children who become orphans are always taken into the families of their relations or friends.' Charity began at home.

42

Paradise Baptist Church

Gravestones, eroded by time and weather, commemorate God-fearing farmers at the Baptist church, West
Paradise, Annapolis Valley. The first new settlers in the
valley that the Acadians had left were mostly New England
land-grabbers, and, as surely as God made the valley's little
green apples, Puritanism coloured their thinking. Puritanism proclaimed every man's Christian duty not only to
earn money but also to choose the work most profitable to
himself. Luxury, extravagance, and too much pleasure
were all unchristian. Diligence, ceaseless activity, sobriety,
thrift, self-discipline, and foresight, however, were decidedly Christian; they also happened to be qualities that
came close to guaranteeing commercial success, or making a go of a farm. Some were dry-footed, like the man in
Charles Bruce's poem *Biography*:

   He was a careful man, a trifle cold
   To meet and talk to. There were some who thought
   His hand was a bit grasping, when he sold;
   A little slow to open when he bought.

   But no one said it that way. When you heard
   His habits mentioned, there would be a pause.
   And then the soft explanatory word.
   They said he was dry-footed. And he was.

Widow's walk, Yarmouth (right)

Nowhere is a widow's walk more appropriate than in
Yarmouth, N.S. From 1831 to 1902, no less than 133
sailing vessels and steamers were wrecked on the shores
of Yarmouth County. The fate of the *City of Monticello*
was typical. A 232-foot passenger steamer, she foundered
on 10 November 1900. She was almost within sight of this
very house. Yet only four men made it safely to shore. She
rolled over and sank. Lifeboats went down with her.
Lifeboats swamped. Lifeboats splintered on the murdering
rocks. Thirty-six perished, and the corpses rolled ashore at
nearby Chebogue Point. Roughly 140 years earlier, Yarmouth's first English-speaking settlers weren't proper Bos-
tonians, but they were certainly proper New Englanders.
They had names like Eleshama Eldredge, Consider Fuller,
Ebenezer Ellis, and Moses Perry. In 1898, a brochure of the
Yarmouth Steamship Company remembered them as
'God-fearing men, who brought with them the name of
Yarmouth. What could be expected from such men, who
were all Pelegs and Seths, Judas and Joshuas, but a community noted for thrift and energy, honesty and uprightness?'
And sailing ability. By the 1870s Yarmouth boasted more
tonnage of sailing vessels, per capita, than any other port in
Canada. 'Up on the hill,' Dorothy Duncan wrote in 1942,
'stand fine old houses, proud of their high ceilings, mahogany furniture, porcelain treasures brought from the Ori-
ent, and widow's walks around the roofs. They remember
how it was.... when famous windjammers and the men
who sailed them were equally proud as they moved out
into a scudding breeze past Yarmouth Light on ventures
that took them wherever cargoes and men's imaginations
called.'

Three churches, Mahone Bay

Mahone Bay is 'the town of churches'–the sand-coloured one is St James Anglican (1833), the white ones are St John's Lutheran (about 1869) and Trinity United (1862)–but the town hasn't always been as tranquil as steeples and still water suggest. Its name comes from *mahonne*, the French word for boats–preferred by pirates–that lay so low in the water they could lurk undetected among hundreds of nearby islands. Pirates not only pounced on shipping, they also attacked the town. In 1782, a privateer waltzed right up the bay, and nabbed a loaded vessel just as she was nudging the town wharf. Names like Murderer's Point and Sacrifice Island–where Indians are said to have offered a white child to a deity–commemorate grisly old times. In 1813, a British man-of-war cornered the Yankee privateer *Young Teazer*. Lieutenant Frederick Johnson, knowing the British would hang him, hurled a torch into *Young Teazer's* gunpowder supply. She blew higher than any steeple, and there's a legend that the vessel still haunts the bay, sometimes as a ship, other times as a ball of fire. The earliest settlers included tough, industrious Germans, and by the late nineteenth century their descendants were prospering on fishing, trade, lumber, and shipbuilding. A slump followed but, in the Prohibition era, rum-running took up some of the slack. These days, the town of churches is also a town of antique shops, and visiting yachtsmen have replaced the visiting pirates.

Lunenburg Harbour

Among dozens of snug seaside towns on the South Shore, the classic fishing village is Lunenburg (population: 3,024). First settled by European farmers who quickly turned to the sea, Lunenburg has long depended for its trade and survival on what its people could pull out of the ocean or carry over the ocean. The sea dominates even its folklore and ghost stories. Lunenburg has a front harbour, a back harbour and, in the centre of town, wooden buildings that remind one of photographs taken when the waterfront was still a forest of masts, and no event was more sad and thrilling than the departure of the schooner fleet for the Grand Banks off Newfoundland. Lunenburg has museum-vessels that celebrate its fishing triumphs and the dubious glory of its rum-runners. But it's not a ghost town. It's still a major fishing port, fish-processor, vessel-builder. For yachts and ships, it makes everything from hammocks, sails, and brassworks, to stoves, dories, and engines. Lunenburg, in short, still lives off the sea.

Young's Cove, Bridgetown

At Young's Cove, on the Fundy Shore, another wooden vessel slowly takes her graceful shape. Such scenes were once routine in every seaside community in the province. In the 1870s, Nova Scotia, New Brunswick, and Prince Edward Island built, owned, and operated a massive fleet of wind-driven wooden merchant ships. These three provinces were the major reason why it was that in 1878 Canada ranked fourth among all the ship-owning countries of the world, with 7,196 vessels totalling 1,333,015 tons. 'They captured a huge share of the world's carrying trade,' Frederick William Wallace wrote in *Wooden Ships and Iron Men*, 'and built up a reputation for smart ships and native-born seamen that was a legend in nautical history and fo'c'sle story for many years.... A little company of ship-builders and sailors resident on the shores of the Atlantic coast of Canada created a mercantile marine which burst into ocean commerce, made history and drew the admiration of seamen, and thence vanished into the mists of oblivion.' When the Age of Sail was finished so were they.

Wooden anchors, Isle Madame; Eel spear, Sherbrooke Village

The spear's for sticking eels. The anchors on Isle Madame look like an archaeologist's find. They're not. Even if the design does go back a century or two, they're working anchors. Tomorrow they'll do their job. Isle Madame is a corner of Cape Breton that's off the track beaten by tourists. Fishermen from St Malo, France, founded D'Escousse, an Isle Madame town, in 1718, and the names on the original land-grant maps still dominate the island. 'Like all of Nova Scotia, D'Escousse flourished in the last century,' Silver Donald Cameron wrote recently. 'By 1881 it boasted 1,492 souls, and a detailed map of 1886 shows half a dozen wharves and stores, a lobster factory, a forge and a hotel. When all the fishing and trading vessels were laid up for the winter, you could walk across the harbor on the decks of the fleet.' Fewer than 300 people live there now.

48

David Stevens; Schooner-building

David Stevens of Second Peninsula, Lunenburg County, never thinks of himself as a custodian of living history – he builds wooden sailing vessels simply because he loves to build wooden sailing vessels – but that's precisely what he is. The history he helps keep alive is schooner history. He's an old-age pensioner, grandfather of nine, loyal husband, non-smoker, non-drinker, milker of his own cows, raiser of his own beef, grower of his own vegetables, man of few words and much land, son of a sailmaker, brother of a sailmaker, brother-in-law of a ship's outfitter, grandson of a shipbuilder, father of a shipbuilder, cousin to four shipbuilders, a master shipbuilder himself, and, as it happens, one heck of a man to face in a schooner race. He's seventy-five. Stevens was born on Tancook Island, which is in the waters he still sails, and had nine brothers and sisters. 'I first started chipping out little models,' he recalled, 'when I was seven or eight years old. That's the designing end of it, I suppose. I was so interested

in it I used to sham sickness to stay home from school. They used to call it 'the nine o'clock sickness' because right after that I'd be fine, and I'd get my mother to go up to the shop – Dad's sail-loft – and get me a nice piece of pine. I got a lot of cut fingers in those days.' Life was tough on Tancook. 'You *had* to be able to build a boat just to get off the island.' Still, Stevens didn't get serious about building boats for money till after the Second World War. Since then, he's built sixty-nine. He 'retired' a dozen years ago, but that only meant he lost interest in building boats for money. He's built half a dozen since then just for the love of it, and in the winter of '82 he was finishing off a twenty-six-foot schooner. That's a good twenty feet shorter than the racing schooners with which he's conquered so many challengers. He thought he'd see what he could do with a smaller vessel because, out on the courses off the South Shore, 'I was beginning to feel like a bully.'

Wooden boatbuilding; Sailmaking

Old skills die hard. Leaving aside the thousands of smaller vessels that Maritimers launched in the Age of Sail, they built and operated nearly eight hundred 'tern schooners'. These were three-, four-, even five-masted cargo vessels that sailed seas the world over. But as Master Mariner John B. Parker put it more than twenty years ago, 'The sail-driven cargo vessel has quietly disappeared from Atlantic Canada, and from all the waters of North America.

Sail has also been discarded by the fishing fleets of both Canada and the United States. The internal-combustion engine has superseded canvas and wind in every phase of commercial seafaring endeavour, and the windships are but a memory.' But not the yachts, and, in a Lunenburg loft, sailmaking survives. Moreover, at workshops in seaside villages like Clark's Harbour, there are still men who can build you a wooden boat from scratch.

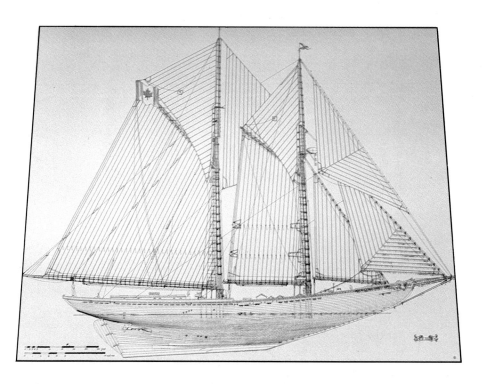

Bluenose II

Sambro Light, N.S. Museum (right)

She was the most famous sailing vessel in the history of Canada. She was the proudest proof of Nova Scotia's sea-faring ability and you can still find her, tiny but beautiful, on the Canadian dime. Her real length was 143 feet. She carried an 81-foot mainmast, a 53½-foot main topmast, roughly 10,000 square feet of sail. She was the *Bluenose*, greatest of all 'Salt Bankers'. From 1921, when Bill Roue designed her and the Lunenburg yard of Smith and Rhuland built her, until her last races in 1938, she never lost a series to the New England challengers in the International Fishermen's Schooner Races. Her skipper was Angus Walters, and his epic battles with rivals out of Gloucester, Mass., made such widespread news they reminded expatriate Nova Scotians everywhere of their heritage. Bluenose poet Charles Bruce wrote, 'Listen to little Angus, squinting at the *Bluenose*:/"The timber that'll beat her still stands in the woods."/Yes, these are the fellows who remind you again of the sea.' She died on a reef off Haiti in 1946 but in 1963, the Oland brewing family of Halifax (see page 79) financed construction of a replica. Owned by the Nova Scotia government now, *Bluenose II* has also sailed close-hauled into the hearts of Nova Scotians. The ink drawing by marine artist L.B. Jenson is part of a portfolio of scale drawings and diagrammatic sketches entitled *The Last of The Tall Schooners.*

The glittering refractive lens of the lantern from the Sambro light has belonged to the Nova Scotia Museum since 1969 but, with a modern beacon to replace it, the 82-foot-high octagonal lighthouse still looks much as it did when the colonial government first built the structure in 1760. It's the oldest lighthouse in use in Canada, and probably in North America. It towers above a small granite island in the treacherous outer approaches to Halifax Harbour. In 1758, Governor Lawrence told London the local legislative council would fund it by taxing 'past imported and retailed spirituous liquors.... Out of the same fund, we are now finishing the inside of the Church.' Liquor taxes, in short, would help save the lives of sailors at sea and the souls of Haligonians on land. A public lottery helped raise more money for the lighthouse. Its early operation was scandalously lax. Often, no one bothered to turn it on. The British admiralty speculated, for instance, that the cause of the *Granby's* sinking in 1771 was 'the want of a light being kept in the Lighthouse at that place.... The captains of His Majesty's ships are frequently obliged to fire at the Lighthouse to make them shew a light.'

Lighthouse, Peggy's Cove (left)

Few lighthouses in the world have been photographed more often than the one at Peggy's Cove, and the village itself rivals the bridges of Paris as a hangout for Sunday painters. The weatherbeaten houses, sheds, and wharves, the fishing boats that nestle in their intimate haven from the roaring Atlantic, and the strange plains of glacier-scraped granite bring visitors to Peggy's Cove from across the continent. In high summer, tourists swarm like ants on the sun-baked stone, but on one wall of the lighthouse there's a tip that horror lurks at the very edge of the picture-postcard setting. A sign reads: 'Warning. Injury and death have rewarded careless sight-seers here. The ocean and rocks are treacherous. Savour the sea from a distance.' Once in a while, a murdering wave snatches a victim from the rock and promptly pulverizes him.

Low tide

Tide's out. But when it rises in the upper reaches of the Bay of Fundy, it rises more than fifty feet, higher than anywhere else in the world. Mountain freshets become surging tidal rivers. Fresh water becomes salt and, later, salt water becomes fresh. Oceans of grass appear, and fields of ocean. In the wink of a day, massive plains of mud disappear under a thousand whitecaps, reappear, disappear again. 'Brag about your country, boys,' nineteenth-century statesman Joseph Howe once urged his fellow Nova Scotians. He went on to say that, when confronted with the glories of other nations, he'd ask, 'How high does your tide rise?'

St Peter's Lighthouse, Brier Island

'To see! To see!' Joseph Conrad, novelist, once wrote. 'This is the craving of the sailor.' To satisfy that craving at the entrance to the frequently treacherous and fog-bound Bay of Fundy, the colonial governments of Nova Scotia and New Brunswick got together in 1807 to vote funds for the construction of St Peter's Lighthouse, Brier Island. The light went into service two years later. By 1810 at least ten lights were winking in Nova Scotian waters, and in 1825 there were ten in the Bay of Fundy alone, and another eight on the Atlantic coast. 'During the big immigration and growth period of the middle and late nineteenth century, the number of Nova Scotia lights trebled,' lighthouse historian Dudley Witney wrote. 'A development in the fueling of lights...was the brainchild of a Nova Scotian, Dr. Abraham Gesner of Cornwallis. In 1846...Gesner produced [kerosene] from coal, and used it in the new lamp in the Maugher Beach lighthouse in Halifax harbour. The light and the new fuel worked so well that the gentle physician made a fortune.' In our own time, more than a thousand lights, beacons, and buoys help vessels safely make their way along Nova Scotia's tricky coast.

Waves

Thomas Raddall, Nova Scotia's eminent author of historical novels, knew what was worthy of fear: 'The sea that could get up and roar; that could make you turn and run, afraid to look over your shoulder; that could overtake you in a stride and rattle you and your mates like so many dice in a cup; that could ram your own breath down your throat, that could slap your face hours on end and put the salt taste of death in your mouth, that could freeze you and soak you and beat the stuffing out of you; that could make you curse the day you ever saw more water than a good morning's dew on the grass.'

Rain (left)

Summer rain spatters beach stones. Often, the whole province appears to be little more than an eternal assault by water on rock. Here, the assault is merely a caress, but it may be the prelude to a widow-making gale. Then again it may not be. The shower may swiftly pass, and the sunshine set the bay glittering again. Weather-forecasting is a tough job in Nova Scotia, and sometimes older folk hopefully explain, 'If you don't like the weather, just wait an hour.' The trouble is, the saying works in reverse, too.

Gulliver's Cove

Gulliver's Cove (population: 93) is on the outer shore of Digby Neck, and that means it's both a victim of the violent tides of the Bay of Fundy, and an exploiter of Fundy's fisheries. Along that shore, author Will R. Bird once explained, 'Always there would be black irregular fences rising from the water, pole and brush markings of weir and trap.' Gulliver's Cove takes its name from 'Cut-Throat Gulliver', a pirate who made it his headquarters. A local man told Bird Gulliver's story: 'Folks hereabout took him a steer, or sheep and hogs whenever he demanded, for his men were a hungry crew and they'd be quick to come with gun and sword, and they'd fire the place if they had any opposition. They tell, too, that his lady was a coloured woman from the West Indies, near six-foot tall and good features. She had earrings with pearls big as chestnuts and a necklace of diamonds. She wore her own knife and pistol, and could speak English as good as Gulliver himself. But she was unhappy in these parts and wanted the warm weather, and when he made too much fun of her she put her knife between his ribs and sailed the ship back to her island, and then handed her over to Gulliver's men. And they tell every man jack of them was scared to death of her, and praying glad when she got from the ship.'

Whale Cove markers; Lobster traps, Sandy Cove

Found sculpture: stacked lobster pots at Sandy Cove, Digby Neck; and, at Whale Cove, Cape Breton, a vivid heap of red markers. Since lobsters are among the world's most expensive gustatory indulgences, older Nova Scotians enjoy recalling when they were so tiresomely plentiful that farmer-fishermen dumped them on their fields as fertilizer. Lobster meat was supposedly fit only for the poverty-stricken, and children begged their mothers not to shame them by forcing them to carry lobster sandwiches to school. Peanut butter was socially preferable. Now, the creature that author Harold Horwood once called 'that great bug from the Canadian sea bottom' is vital to the economic survival of hundreds of Nova Scotian families. For, in the worshipful opinion of a Canadian fisheries officer, *Homarus americanus* is 'the most highly prized animal in the sea and, indubitably, the undisputed divine monarch of the Royal Family of Seafoods…the absolute favorite of connoisseurs, gourmets, epicures and bon vivants the world over as the most delectable of dishes.' And those lobster pots, which seal the great bugs' doom, are not only the ubiquitous symbols of a multimillion-dollar industry but also treasured souvenirs. They go west on the rooftops of countless cars, and grace recreation rooms in cattle country a thousand miles from the smell of the sea.

Assorted nets; Scallop shells

The nets are for assorted ground fish. The scallop shells, taken individually, are perhaps the fishing industry's most beautiful debris. Indians and settlers used them as dishes, cooking utensils, and ornaments; and seaside smokers still regard them as the ocean's best ashtrays. Scallops are filter-feeding herbivores. Their elaborate gills act as sieves to trap food. A scallop has a heart, mouth, stomach, intestine, and kidney, but no head. The mantle – a membrane that surrounds the body and builds the shell out of lime – has a fringe with tentacles and roughly a hundred eyes. The eyes can just detect an approaching predator. The scallop escapes by jet propulsion. A powerful muscle opens the shells to receive water, then snaps

them shut, ejecting the water and shooting the scallop as far as fourteen feet. Though Europeans eat almost the entire creature, it's only that one white, meaty muscle that's marketed in North America. Our fish business treats the rest of this complex being as offal. It's that small, expensive muscle that, for years now, has had the United States and Canada bickering and bargaining over boundaries and quotas in the great scallop grounds off New England and Nova Scotia. Meanwhile, Digby, N.S., still boasts one of the world's biggest scallop fleets, and wherever seafood-lovers gather, 'Digby scallops' are a synonym for succulence.

Whale Cove; Slipway

Y ou needn't visit a museum to find the old Nova Scotia. These scenes happen to be at Whale Cove, on the west coast of Cape Breton Island, but the ingredients are the same in a hundred other spots, and have been for a

long time. Whitecaps on the bay, a wooden shack, a dirt road, lobster pots among wildflowers, and a slipway that, for all its apparent crudeness, works as it has always worked.

Sherbrooke Village postmistress; Postal scales

Like much of Nova Scotia, Sherbrooke had a brief Golden Age in the nineteenth century, and then – for various political, economic, and technological reasons – drifted into a long sleep of decline. Named after Sir John Coape Sherbrooke, Lieutenant-Governor of Nova Scotia from 1811 to 1816, Sherbrooke enjoyed its good times from 1860 to the 1880s. It's at the head of tide on the St Mary's River, the Eastern Shore, and what lured the earliest white settlers to the spot were massive stands of tall pines that surrounded the salmon-rich river. Sherbrooke thrived on shipbuilding and lumber, exporting wood as far away as Britain and the West Indies. Then, in 1861, two little sisters found some pretty stones while picking blueber-

ries. Their father took these 'garden decorations' to a metallurgist in Halifax, and soon prospectors were crawling all over the blueberry patch. That, at least, is one story of how Sherbrooke's short-lived gold rush began. By 1869, nineteen mining companies had settled in the area, and merchants reaped a flash of prosperity. Government has now turned part of Sherbrooke into a restoration which, though not exactly a gold mine, is certainly making cash registers jingle. The Sherbrooke Village Restoration gives visitors a chance to roam a flourishing town as it was a century ago and, among other things, to buy stamps from a period postmistress at a period post office.

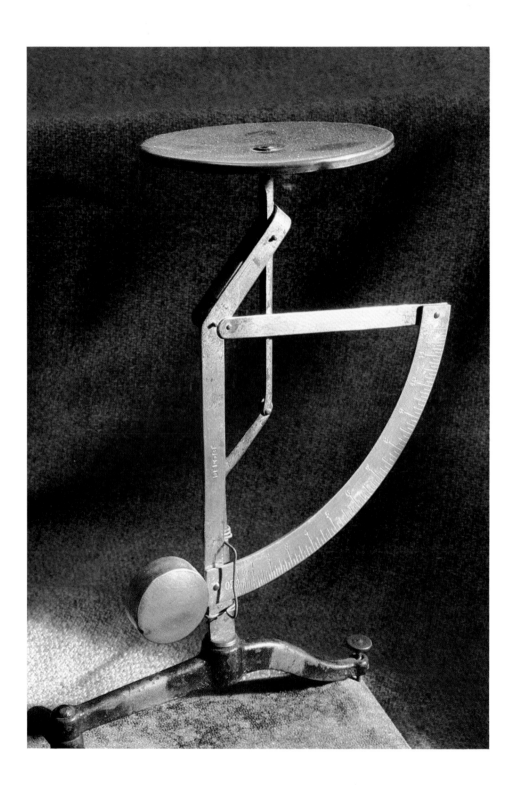

Sherbrooke Village chemist's shop

The old chemist's shop is a favourite hangout for visitors to the Sherbrooke Village Restoration who want to get a feeling for nineteenth-century shopping. The village, however, includes other wooden testaments to the way things were in a bustling Nova Scotia town in the 1870s: a blacksmith shop, boat-building shop, tea room,

general store, printing plant, and a dozen other rebuilt establishments. Costumed guides encourage visitors to take a crack at nineteenth-century crafts and tasks. The guides, incidentally, are mostly Sherbrooke people. Their own ancestors perfected the crafts and performed the tasks, not for show but for survival.

Mills House

Back in the mid-1800s, during the palmy days of ship-building and deep-sea navigation, a man named George Mills built a pretty house at Granville Ferry. It looked across Annapolis Basin toward Annapolis Royal, and among its features was a superbly crafted hanging staircase. It's still there. Mrs R.E. Carlson of Massachusetts, the builder's great-granddaughter, restored the house. 'At this place the river is wide and extremely rapid,' Thomas Chandler Haliburton (see page 39) wrote in 1829, 'but on account of the eddies which form on both sides of it, it is passed with ease.' You passed it with ease on a ferry run by Harris and Lawrence Hall, enterprising brothers who also owned a livery stable and a licensed inn or 'house of entertainment'. You could sleep and eat there for sixteen cents a night. The Halls raised cattle and sold meat to the garrison at Fort Anne. Since they were also the chief liquor merchants in the county, they no doubt sold a fair bit of booze to the soldiers as well.

Barrington Woollen Mill

The Barrington Woollen Mill, a museum now, operated commercially from 1884 right down to 1962. It was the last of at least twenty small woollen factories in Nova Scotia, and an heir to a local woollen-making tradition that stretched back to before the American Revolution. Fishermen from Cape Cod and Massachusetts began to settle Barrington in 1761, and they brought sheep with them. They needed tough, warm clothing, and on the nearby headlands and islands their sheep could graze year-round with little fencing. June was shearing time out on the islands, and an old man once recalled, 'I learned to shear when I was ten, and from that time the Shearing Day Picnic was no fun for me. The women set up tables or put a tablecloth on the grass, and prepared lunch. One day we were late getting the sheep yarded, so we only grabbed a sandwich at noon.... Late in the afternoon, two ladies brought us sandwiches. We couldn't take time to wash. They fed us by hand while we hurried to get the last few sheep sheared before the tide ebbed.' To get off the island, they had to catch the tide. Nor was the mill a place for the lazy. In the 1880s, work began at 7 a.m. and, with an hour off for lunch, ended at 6.15 p.m. The company outlawed not only 'scuffling or boisterous conduct' but also 'talking', or leaving the floor without the foreman's permission. Moreover, 'Any person wishing to speak with an employee must first get permission from the person in charge.' The mill's wool was good, right to the end.

Barrel-making; Quilting

The barrel-maker is at work at Ross Farm, and the quilt-maker is practising her old craft at the Sherbrooke Village Restoration. In the small towns of Nova Scotia, there was a time in which dozens of men and women had skills that were essential to everyone's well-being. There was nothing artsy-craftsy about their work. Making quilts, barrels, buckets, horseshoes, rakes, axe handles, and the other implements of daily survival was a matter of just that: survival. The age of plastic and factory-produced ugliness made the skill and loving care of these villagers obsolete but, here and there, the hands remember. They keep on doing what they've always done best. The farm families

were even more self-sufficient than the villagers. In the first half of the nineteenth century, historian J.B. Calkin once wrote, 'The settler built his own house, barn and pig-pen; he made his...carts, sleds, harrows, yokes, rakes, baskets, barrels, milk dishes, cheese presses, brooms.... The house was by turns a cheese factory, a soap factory, a candle factory, a carding mill, a spinning jenny, a weaving mill.... From the sheep raised on the farm the wool was shorn, and then picked, carded, spun, woven, and made into garments.... In the attic were stored the home-grown medicinal herbs from which, with mortar and pestle, various concoctions for the sick were made.'

Entrance to Haliburton House (left)

Acacia, beech, maple, juniper, and poplar trees flanked the long driveway that led to Thomas Chandler Haliburton's house, Clifton (see also page 39). He and his wife, Louisa, loved the place, and worked hard to make it suitable for his lavish entertaining. They planted fruit trees, hedges, flowers. They built nooks and benches among the shrubs. But Louisa died in 1841, the same year that Haliburton became a Supreme Court judge. In 1856, he closed Clifton, resigned his judgeship, and moved to London. He remarried there, and won a seat in the British Parliament but, like other writers, he was wittier with his pen than he was on his feet. 'He crossed verbal swords with Gladstone more than once,' Dorothy Duncan wrote in 1942, 'and always came off badly in the encounters.' He died in 1865, but the creation of his days at Clifton, Sam Slick, still has his fans.

Door on Hollis Street

This house on Hollis Street, Halifax, is a rarity. It preserves in stone the residential elegance of the past but, the truth is, Hollis was becoming a commercial avenue as far back as the 1760s. 'Halifax was prosperous,' Thomas Raddall wrote, 'and growing beyond the rickety old palisades like a lusty wench bursting out of an old tight bodice.' Just up the slope, Argyle and Grafton were becoming fashionable residential streets. They're now part of the city's commercial heartland, too, and the posh housing lies a couple of miles south on the shores of the yacht-sprinkled Northwest Arm. That territory, in the early days, was still a dark, trackless forest, fit only for bears and Indians.

Halifax explosion memorial

This dark, stark sculpture is a memorial to the victims of a dark, stark event. On 6 December 1917, the *Mont Blanc*, a French freighter carrying 2,500 tons of explosives, collided with a Norwegian ship in Halifax Harbour, caught fire, and exploded. The blast unleashed a man-made force that, until the atomic bomb, was the most destructive in world history. No one will ever know the exact toll, but the official figures were 1,963 killed, 9,000 injured, 199 blinded. For decades after, Halifax had more than its share of nervousness about munitions shipments, and more than its share of disfigured townsfolk. But Mrs Wilbert Swindells, a cheerful grandmother from whom the explosion stole an eye when she was only eight, typifies the spirit of the survivors. Remembering the slaughter of her mother, her two little sisters, and a brother, and remembering her own good right eye, she said, 'Thank God for small mercies.'

Mont Blanc's anchor; Head on St Paul's window

People saw and heard the explosion more than fifty miles away. British author Michael J. Bird said it had 'the violence of a hundred typhoons,' and turned north-end Halifax into 'a vast burning scrapyard, over which hung an enormous billowing cloud.' He said, 'Churches, schools, shops, factories and houses alike caved in, or burst into clouds of flying wreckage.' An entire square mile of Halifax was laid waste 'as completely as if a closely packed army of bulldozers had passed over it.' In addition to the death, blindness, and human disfigurement the blast caused, it left 25,000 Haligonians without decent shelter. If any good arose from this horrendous event it was that author Hugh MacLennan worked it into *Barometer Rising*, perhaps the first truly Canadian novel. Its evidence survives, too, in the half-ton shank of the *Mont Blanc's* anchor, which still lies where it landed, two miles from the explosion on the far side of the Northwest Arm; and in the strange hole blown in a window of St Paul's Church (see page 22). The hole so closely resembles a man's profile that the church has preserved it within double panes.

Premier's office (left)

Inlaid with seashells and topped by a picture of the schooner *Bluenose*, the fireplace in the Premier's office at Province House celebrates the sea and breathes political history. Province House, opened in 1819, is the oldest legislative building in Canada and, in some expert opinion, the nation's finest example of Georgian architecture. It was here that Joseph Howe not only made his historic speech in defence of freedom of the colonial press, but also led the fight that in 1848 resulted in Nova Scotia's becoming the first British colony to achieve responsible government. The chamber of the Legislative Assembly, which has rung with political debate for 163 years, is among the prettiest, most intimate rooms of its kind in Canada. When Charles Dickens visited Halifax in 1842, he said the nearby Red Chamber reminded him of the British House of Commons, seen through the wrong end of a telescope.

Halifax Breweries, Ltd. calendar

'Our fall brewings are now in splendid condition', boasts a calendar from Halifax Breweries, Ltd. in February 1897. The managing director was John C. Oland, a member of a family that began to brew ale in the 1860s and has been at it ever since. John James Dunn Oland, a Cambridge-educated English country gentleman, his wife Susannah, and their seven children all arrived in Halifax in 1864. Oland had come to help run the new Nova Scotia Railway, but 'the good brown October ale' that Mrs Oland and her sons made soon became so famous the family plunged into the brewing business. Three years later, a riding accident killed the senior Oland. His wife had left a comfortable estate in Hampshire, and a place in English society. She had become a brewer in a raw, cold colony. She'd lost her husband. But she now proved herself to be anything but a demure, self-effacing Victorian mother. Susannah firmly took the brewery's reigns. It became S. Oland Sons and Company, and remained that way for a quarter century. Despite major fires, prohibition, and the destruction of its plant by the Halifax explosion (see page 76), later generations of Olands kept the business not only alive but expanding. Victor deB. Oland served as Lieutenant-Governor from 1968 to 1973. The lady brewer of Victorian Nova Scotia knew how to found a dynasty as well as make beer.

Apple harvest

By the 1920s, Nova Scotia's annual commercial apple crop surpassed two million barrels. 'In the light of every sort of justice, including poetic justice, the Annapolis Valley is the fit and proper scene for Canada's first apple blossom festival,' the *Kentville Advertiser* bragged. 'Nature and Man and Time and Tide have made it so. "Thy mouth is a snow apple," sang a poet who knew and loved all this Acadian apple land. . . . It is Annapolis Valley poetry. Our poets do not always stick to their apples. . . . But who ever heard of a poet being inspired by bananas, or even oranges?' No apple valley ever had a more passionate supporter than the *Advertiser*. It reported that the ancient Norse knew apples were the rejuvenating food of their gods, and also that, 'Sojourners in tropical lands, bespattered with the juices and cloyed with the pulp of strange fruits, long for the juicy, tangy crispness of a northern apple.'

Huckleberry leaves

If the apple harvest has symbolized autumn's tang since the beginning of settlement, so have flaming outbursts of huckleberry leaves. They're less useful, but no less beautiful. And you don't have to pick them.

Child's bouquet; Granny's loving hands

There is history in generation after generation of Nova Scotians whose signatures you'll never find on any treaty, whose portraits you'll never find in any museum, whose names you'll never find in any book.